Connections:

body, mind, spirit

written and designed by
terri hoyland

First printing, May 1993
by Terri Hoyland

Printed in the United States of America

ISBN 1-883794-21-X

Printed by Pepco Litho, Inc, Cedar Rapids, Iowa
Published by Heartlights Imagery, Inc.
P.O. Box 36
Cedar Rapids, Iowa 52402

connections:

body, mind, spirit

written and designed by
terri hoyland

Dear Friend,

These pages were deliberately left untouched to remind us all of our many imperfections and humanness.

We hope you look beyond the mere words to seek their true meaning and see your own reflection. The hand written texts remain in that form so that you may identify with them just as if you had written them yourself.

Any references to "man" in quotes remains as originally written by the author. Our interpretation of what it means to us is expanded beyond the literal interpretation of the meaning of the word "man" to include <u>all</u> men and women.

Peace be with you on your journey,
Heartlights Imagery

P. O. Box 36
Cedar Rapids, Iowa 52406
(319) 366-2041

This book is dedicated to...
Michael, my parter in love...
my sister, Mary, whose love and affection
keeps me going and growing,...
Amy and Gina, my adopted "daughters",
who teach me about love beyond blood, ...
Carmen, my lifelong friend, ...
Nancy and Dianne, my business partners.

These connections reflect so many facets of life
and I am forever grateful for all that you are.

I understand

I understand the seasons.
the Glory.
the Death
the Resurrection
the Peace
I understand winter's rest
to appreciate the soul for spring's celebration...
daffodils' power to push through frozen soil.

I understand purple.
I understand the labor of planting...
the visualization of the harvest.

The summer heat invites gnats to suck on my neck,
as sweat leaks from my temple,
I understand the heat and the gentle breeze that teases me.

I hear growth.
I understand green
I understand the autumn...
fullness touching the harvest.

I understand the death of leaves.
Orange all around me demanding to be seen
and then flutter to their maker, the soil.

The earth gets ready for bed.
I understand winter's white.
the Night
the Angels
the Peace

Dianne Brown Ross

"The
kingdom
of
God
is

within
you."

Luke 17:21

The divine plan is beyond my understanding.
Yet I know I am part of this plan.
Inside of myself
is a place where I draw understanding.
Each breath I take connects me to God.

I breathe in resourcefulness and
breathe out wastefulness.
I breathe in beauty and
breathe out shame.
I breathe in wisdom and
breathe out stupidity.
I breathe in energy and
breathe out apathy.
I breathe in respect and
breathe out the need to be judgemental.
I breathe in harmony and
breathe out chaos.
I breathe in love and
breathe out anger.

WITHIN ME IS THE KEY TO
PEACE AND UNDERSTANDING.

"The best way
to know God
is to
love
many things."

Van Gogh

God is all around me in everything I feel, smell, see, hear and experience.

I am open to seeing things through God's eyes:
sunshine caressing my skin
blades of grass tickling my feet
rainbows bringing tenderness and forgiveness
thunderstorms cleaning up the air
tree trunks that support their fruit
mountain tops glowing with awesome majesty
bees making sweet sustenance
flowers clothed in fragile beauty
children playing in the absence of worry

What I do today and where I go teach me about God:
customers provide a need I can fulfill
computers are a product of human knowledge
home is a safe harbor
art is a reflection of inner creativity
football is working together with power and strength.

Each thing reflects a different facet of God's divine power.
When I love these things, I learn more about God.
The more I learn,
the more I understand.

WITH LOVE, I KNOW GOD.

"*God-*
that unity of bests."

Elizabeth Barrett Browning

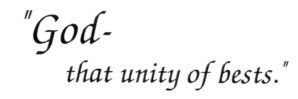

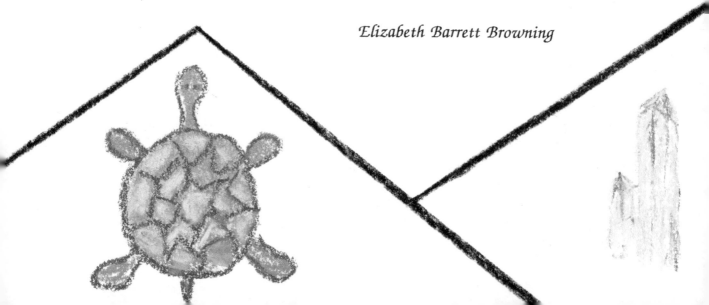

I believe God created a perfect world,
a world that brings together
all the best of life.

I understand God when I also am my best
like when I love others unconditionally,
appreciate nature's cyclical refrains,
accept differences without judgement,
rejoice in the beauty around me.

My thoughts and actions unite to create my best self.
I act in ways that maintain God's perfect world:
I work to keep the water pure and air clean,
I preserve the land and respect the laws of nature.
I strive for harmony with the world.

When I do these things, I know God.

I UNDERSTAND GOD'S BEST.

"Let us live in
peace and harmony to keep the
land and all life in balance.
Only prayer and meditation
can do that."

Thomas Banyacka
Wisdomkeepers

It is not enough that I think
that peace and harmony are important.
It is essential that I <u>act</u> in ways
that create peace,
that I live a lifestyle that encourages harmony.

Through prayer,
I ask for strength and energy to live a peaceful life.
Through meditation,
I find the wisdom to act accordingly.

I AM THE SUM TOTAL OF
MY THOUGHTS AND ACTIONS.

"To see the World in a grain of sand
And a Heaven in a wild flower
Hold infinity in the palm of your hand
and eternity in an hour."

William Blake

As I go through this day,
I will live in this moment.
It is all there might be
and embodies all that exists.
I see this very moment through eyes that truly see,
ears that truly hear,
mouth that truly tastes,
and fingers and toes that truly feel.

I open my heart and all my senses open wider.
This moment is more vibrantly alive.
This moment is more vivid and real.

Nothing else matters except this moment,
Certainly not the past nor the future,
only how I live right now.

I AM ALIVE IN MY WORLD.

"I
a m
a
part
of
all
that
I
have
me t."

Alfred Lord Tennyson

There is no such thing as
an insignificant interaction.
We leave a part of ourselves behind.

When I smile at another, I become a
part of that person's day.
   May I make their day happier.

Every business transaction I conduct makes me
an instrumental part of the outcome.
      May I always be ethical.

Every good deed I do serves to provide
hope to another.
      May I reach out to those in need.

Everytime I believe another will succeed,
their success becomes my success.
      MAY I instill in others a good reputation
   to live up to.

I cannot hide behind the belief of insignificance,
   for I am not.
Every word, deed, and thought binds us together
   you and I.

MAY I CHERISH YOU! IN SO DOING,
I HELP CREATE A BEAUTIFUL WORLD.

"In one drop of water
are found the secrets
of all the endless oceans"

Kahlil Gibran

When I look at myself, I see everyone else in the world.
When I see my own beauty, I can see beauty in others.
When I am generous, I look around and see others
    who are also generous.
When I feel at peace, I feel harmony all around.
When I touch others with kindness,
        I see others who extend kindness as well.

Likewise when I feel insecure,
    I recognize that struggle in others.
When I pull back from others,
    I recognize others who also pull away and hide behind walls.

All that I am and hope to be is there in those around me.
        They are just like me —
                filled with their own goodness
                and filled with their own fears.

        My reflection is also theirs.

When I stop and really see their reflection
    I can better understand all people.
So it is in understanding the universe.
What we learn from one leaf, one deer, one star
        we learn about all.

I APPRECIATE ONENESS THROUGH
BEING AND UNDERSTANDING ME.

"We were such a good
and loving invention.
An aeroplane made from a man and woman
Wings and everything.
We hovered a little above the earth.

We even flew a little."

Yelinda Anichar
Wings of Joy

What a delicate balance we need
    in order to rise above –
    that perfect combination of
    masculine and feminine energy.

I cherish my intuition to believe it is possible,
    my ability to feel,
    my compassion to accept
    my imagination to dream how...

I cherish also my ability to take action
    my courage to try
    my logic to overcome obstacles
    my perseverance to keep at it...

I AM PERFECT BY MYSELF.

I welcome you as part of my life.

    Come fly with me –
    you with your perfect combination of
    masculine and feminine energy –
    rising far above earthly understanding
                    and experience...

THE GOSPEL ACCORDING TO SHUG

"HELPED are those whose every act
is a prayer for harmony in the
Universe, for they are the restorers
of balance to one planet.
To them will be given the insight
that every good act done in the
cosmos welcomes the life of an
animal or a child."

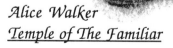

Alice Walker
Temple of The Familiar

There are times when I feel you've hurt me
and I want you to pay for the pain I feel.

If I retaliate to get back at you,
I think I win because you feel pain
but I really lose because I am allowing
my ego to take over and my ego right then
was stronger than my true goodness.

In the quiet of my heart, I know this situation
brings me a lesson on life:

It may bring me an opportunity to feel my own strength
and learn no one can help me but myself.
It may bring me an opportunity to see my own beauty
and learn I am special and unique unto myself.
It may bring me an opportunity to touch my own soul
and learn I can only control myself.
It may bring me an opportunity to free my own spirit
and learn I can rise above the chaos around myself.

MAY I LEARN ABOUT THE JUST AND MERCIFUL ME.

"What, sir, would the people of the earth be without woman?

They would be mighty scarce, sir, mighty scarce."

Mark Twain

I thank God for women
for without them,
we would cease to exist.

I thank God for their wombs
for they bring forth life.

I thank God for their hearts
for they share love and compassion.

I thank God for their minds
for they bring a different point of view.

I thank God for their hands and arms
for they hold babes to their chest.

I thank you, woman, for being.

"No partner in a love relationship...
should feel that he has to give up
an essential part of himself to
make it viable."

Mary Sarton

So what is love?

Love is seeing you as you really are,
   filled with wonderful qualities and many faults
   and loving everything about you.
It is accepting you as you are.
   even when I don't like it.
      For if I truly love you, I love the whole you,
         not just part of you.

When I love you, I don't want to change you.

I will not ask you to give up any part of yourself
   even in the name of love,
      because I have no right to ask you
      to be less than you want.

It is your choice and I respect your choice.
That is an essential aspect of loving you.

I ACCEPT EVERY PART OF YOU.

*"A great man
is he
who does not lose
his child's heart."*

Mencius

I thank you, great and good man,
for all you do-
    for pushing me to be better
    for working so hard
    for providing for more than yourself
    for supporting my endeavors.

I thank you, great and good man,
for all you are-
    for being there when I need you
    for listening when I cry
    for sitting with me when I am sick
    for sharing in my happiness ... and sadness
    for loving me even when I'm not easy to love.

For me,
    your greatness cannot be measured by money,
        but by giving your heart.
    Your goodness cannot be measured by deeds done,
        but by being gentle and kind.

GREAT AND GOOD MAN,
    YOU LIVE FOREVER IN MY HEART.

"Some people come into our lives-
leave footprints on our hearts,
and we are never, ever the same."

Flavia

I appreciate you for bringing me the opportunity...

   to love
   to accept
   to be vulnerable
   to understand and grow
   to forgive

You and I share something special together
   constantly changing as time goes on.

I expose to you my feelings of joy, hope, passion
   as well as pain, hurt, frustration, disappointment.
The more you impact my life
   the more feelings I experience.
The deeper our relationship grows,
   the more honest and open I become.

   What a wonderful experience!
      I can be real.
      I can be myself.
You have brought a beautiful new dimension
into my life.

      I am now different because of you.

   THANK YOU FOR BEING IN MY LIFE.

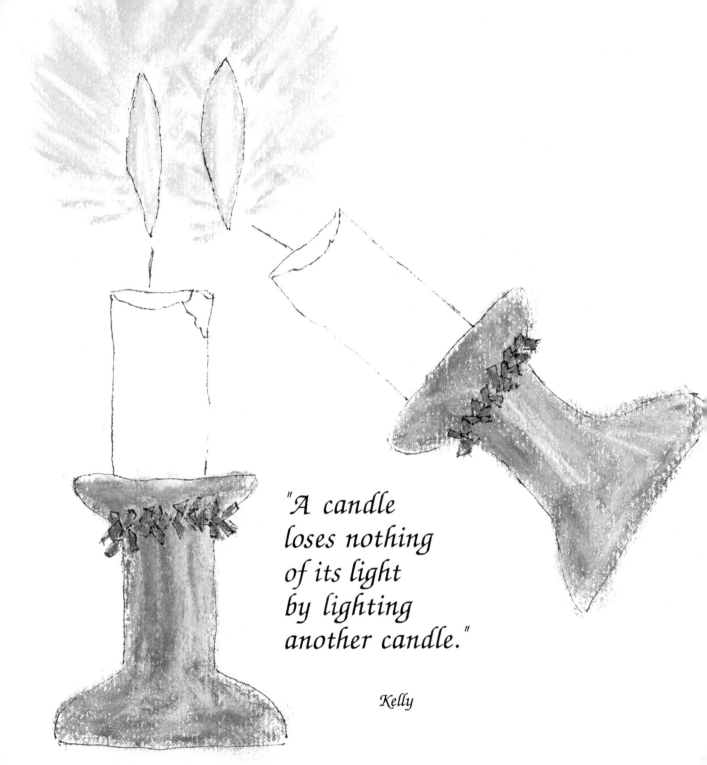

"A candle
loses nothing
of its light
by lighting
another candle."

Kelly

JUST FOR TODAY
   I will seek out some good quality
      in another person
   or share credit for a job well done
      with another.

JUST FOR TODAY
   I will look for you doing something right
   or give you something fun to do.

JUST FOR TODAY
   I will make the way easier
   for someone else.

I will lighten your day by my deeds
knowing it takes nothing away from me.
when I reach out to you.

In fact, with your light and mine,
   I see easier and further.

*"When you truly grow up,
what you will be is free."*

Emanuel

When I am a child,
   I need others to take care of me,
      provide for me.
When I grow up,
   I no longer need others.
I take responsibility for myself and my happiness.
I choose my own way.

I   AM   FREE.

I choose who I live with,
          how I live
          what I do
          where I go
          how much I give or take.
I choose whether or not to spend my life with you,
                          work with you
                          care about you.

No one can make me.
   It is my choice.
      So when I love you, I give you this gift freely.

I FREELY CHOOSE TO LOVE YOU.

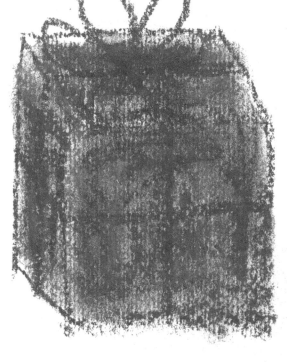

"Whatever is best for our collective future, we will discover it by looking with clear eyes at what made love possible in our individual pasts."

Gloria Steinem
Revolution From Within

Every situation and circumstance in my life
has brought me an opportunity to learn.

When I look beyond the pain, the hurt, the loss,
I see why I loved in the first place.

When I remember why I loved then,
and with a loving heart, what I learned then,
I learn how to love you more fully today.

I see love through new eyes.
I give you love anew and changed
for it is more understanding,
wiser,
accepting,
free...

MY PAST IS A GIFT OF LOVE ANEW.

"In that instant I could feel no doubt
of man's oneness with the universe.
The conviction comes that the rhythm was
too orderly, too harmonious, too perfect
to be a blind chance- that, therefore, there
must be a purpose in the whole and that
man was part of that whole and not an
accidental offshoot."

Admiral Byrd's Diary

I sit in the aloneness of my room
aware of everything around me.
I feel the wind blow kisses against my face.
I hear the birds chirp and sing of another glorious day.
I see the clouds moving so proudly through the sky.
I smell the essence of the lilacs.
I taste the humidity as it lingers all around me.

I and my environment are in harmony.
I am part of this world
no less and no more than any other part.

My mind doesn't understand this divine oneness but
my heart feels all is well.
I feel such joy in this space
knowing I am not really alone.

I AM AT PEACE IN THIS ONENESS.

"How can we buy and sell the sky,
the warmth of the land? The idea is
strange to us. If we do not own the
freshness of the air and the sparkle of
the water, how can we buy them?
We are all part of the Earth, and it is
part of us. The rocky crests, the juices
of the meadows, the body heat of the pony,
and man - all belong to the same family."

Chief Seattle

The most beautiful aspects of life cannot be bought.

I look in awe at the sunsets.
I feel sunlight caress my face.
I lift my eyes toward the moon and stars.
I feel sand sift through my fingers and toes.
I watch the graceful deer dance in the woods.
I smell the wild flowers.
I pick the fruit of the trees.
I drink the flowing water.

I am renewed.
I am refreshed and energized.

BECAUSE THEY ARE, I AM.

"Now I realize
that the trees blossom
in Spring,
and bear fruit
in Summer
without seeking praise,
and they
drop their leaves
in Autumn
and become naked
in Winter
without fearing blame."

Kahlil Gibran

When I finally take away
my mask and expose
my real self,
     I am ready to bloom.

I PRAISE THE WINTERTIME
FOR IT BRINGS THE PROMISE
   OF HOPE AND JOY.

"If there is righteousness in the heart
    there will be beauty in the character.
If there be beauty in the character,
    there will be harmony in the home.
If there is harmony in the home,
    there will be order in the nation.
If there is order in the nation,
    there will be peace in the world."

Author Unknown

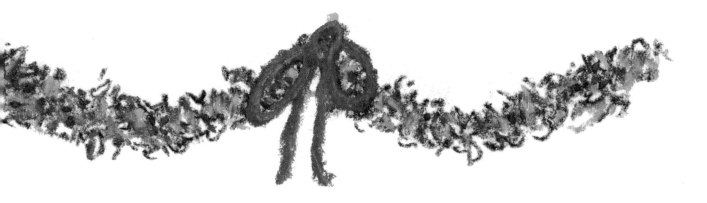

Peace in the world begins with me.
I strive not to be right but to be pure of heart.
I will do my part to bring harmony
        to all my relationships.

I see you and me as two separate people,
        who have much to gain from each other
        and much to give to each other.

I learn from our differences.
        I celebrate our similarities.
                I triumph in our victories.
                        I overcome our challenges.

I honor the you, the me, the we.

I BRING PEACE TO OUR WORLD.

"The truest end of life is
to know that life never ends...
Death is no more than a turning
of us over from time to eternity."

William Penn

Sometimes I fear what I don't understand and
I don't understand death.
Many have come before me and
many will come after.
I came into this world filled
with curiosity and wonder.
I experience joy, hope, love, as well as pain and suffering.

I learn life's lessons sometimes easily,
sometimes with difficulty.
Still, I'm learning.

There will come a time when I'll grow weary
and will be ready for a peaceful rest.

I will hand over this light for someone else
to take with calm acceptance -
and maybe even exuberance,
for my journey is finished...
and theirs is ready to begin.

ALL IS WELL IN OUR WORLD.

"Depart, then, without fear
        of this world,
even as you came into it.
The same way you come
from death to life,
return from life to death.

            Yield your torch to others
            as in a race.
            Your death is but a piece
            of the world's order
            and a parcel of the World's life."

                    Michel de Montaigne

If death brings the promise of bliss ever after,
    then why do I feel fear?
If death is filled with the sweetness of everlasting love,
    why do I feel sad?
If death provides us with all the answers
    why do I not believe?

In my humanness, I can only trust
what I can see and touch myself.
Yet, there are times when I believe the illogical –
        that rainbows bring fresh hopes and new beginnings
        that dreams can come true
        that angels watch over us.
        that prayers can be answered
        that you might really love the imperfect me.
If I can believe in these things,
    maybe I can believe in eternity.
        This life is far beyond my comprehension,
            and far beyond my comprehension in
                connecting life and death.
    I allow my heart to believe...

            I AM PART OF ETERNITY.

To order *Heartlights* **products:**

	Price	Quantity	Total
Heartlights			
Reflections of the love within your heart			
Garden Sojourn			
Guided journey tape	$ 9.98		
Musical journey tape	$ 9.98		
Book of quotes & affirmations	$14.00		
Voyages			
Learning to expand beyond our limitations			
Finding courage and imagination to take			
control of our lives			
Guided journey tape	$ 9.98		
Musical journey tape	$ 9.98		
Book of quotes & affirmations	$14.00		
Connections			
Feel oneness with nature and God			
Understand our relationship with others			
Guided journey tape	$ 9.98		
Musical journey tape	$ 9.98		
Book of quotes & affirmations	$14.00		
Sub-total			
Tax (Iowa only - 5%)			
Shipping & handling			$ 4.00
TOTAL			

Send order to:

Heartlights Imagery, Inc.

P. O. Box 36
Cedar Rapids, Iowa 52406
(319) 366-2041

SHIP TO:
    Name _____
    Address_____
    _____
    Phone (   ) _____

PAYMENT METHOD:
    ___ check   ____ Mastercard   ___ Visa
    _ _ _ _ _ _ _ _ _ _ _ _ _ _ _ Exp ____

Notes for my own quotes and affirmations:

Notes for my own quotes and affirmations:

Notes for my own quotes and affirmations:

Notes for my own quotes and affirmations:

Notes for my own quotes and affirmations:

Notes for my own quotes and affirmations: